She Persisted

in Science

*Brilliant Women
Who Made a
Difference*

I attribute my success to this:

I never gave or took an excuse. • I early

conceived a liking for, and sought every opportunity to relieve

the sufferings of others. • I don't think there is any place in the

world where a woman can't venture. • If you do something once, people will call

it an accident. If you do it twice, they call it a coincidence. But do it a third time and you've just proven a natural law! •

Science and everyday life cannot and should not be separated. • When you're working every day, you're not thinking, 'What impact

is this going to have on the world?' You're thinking, 'I've got to get this right.' • Every one of us makes a difference . . . how we act each day can begin to

change the world. • It adds to the joy of discovery to know that your work may make a difference in people's lives. • What has given my life meaning is more than doing science;

it's helping people solve problems using science. Doing something that makes a difference with what I've learned. • I used to not like being called a woman architect. But I see the

incredible amount of need from other women for reassurance that it could be done, so I don't mind that at all. • Don't be afraid to reach for the stars. • You're never too young or

too small to change the world. • The world . . . should be full of people raising their voices, using their power and presence, standing up for what's right. • If you don't act, we will! •

No child should grow up not knowing what clean water is or never know what running water is. • We showed that we are united and that we, young people, are unstoppable.

Written by
Chelsea Clinton

Illustrated by
Alexandra Boiger

PHILOMEL BOOKS

PHILOMEL BOOKS
An imprint of Penguin Random House LLC, New York

First published in the United States of America by Philomel Books,
an imprint of Penguin Random House LLC, 2022

Library of Congress Cataloging-in-Publication Data is available.

Printed in the USA

ISBN 9780593353295

10 9 8 7 6 5 4 3 2 1

PC

Edited by Jill Santopolo
Design by Ellice M. Lee
Text set in ITC Kennerley

The art was done in watercolor and ink on Fabriano paper, then edited in Photoshop.

To Jasper, Aidan, Charlotte and curious kids everywhere —C. C.

To Heidi, with love —A. B.

Being a woman in science isn't always easy. Sometimes women are told that their ideas aren't smart enough, their research isn't good enough and their work isn't important enough— simply because they're women. But that is not true. The world needs everyone's scientific discoveries.

These women persisted
to prove that to every generation.

As a girl, FLORENCE NIGHTINGALE dreamed of being a nurse. Even though her family didn't agree, she persisted in becoming one. When the British government asked Florence to improve hospital care for soldiers, the staff did not want to listen to a woman. **She persisted** again, and soon hospitals were applying clean bandages to wounds, bathing patients and providing healthy meals. Her habit of walking the wards at night carrying a small light led to her nickname: "Lady with the Lamp." She dedicated her life to improving medical care for patients and training for nurses. Students all over the world still study her methods to improve public health today.

I attribute my success to this:
I never gave or took an excuse.

REBECCA LEE CRUMPLER grew up with her aunt in Pennsylvania and saw how often she cared for their sick neighbors. Inspired, Rebecca became a nurse and then enrolled at the New England Female Medical College, the first school in the United States to train women to be doctors. After becoming the United States' first Black woman doctor, she cared for low-income women and children and then, after the Civil War, worked at the Freedmen's Bureau to care for people who had been enslaved. In the South, Rebecca faced intense racism and sexism. Some of her fellow physicians refused to work with her. She could have given up, but **she persisted** in caring for her patients, knowing many white doctors would refuse to treat them. Her legacy lives on in the Rebecca Lee Society for Black women doctors.

I early conceived a liking for, and sought every opportunity to relieve the sufferings of others.

YNES ENRIQUETTA JULIETTA MEXIA

and her family moved often when she was growing up. The few constants in her life were her love of reading, of exploring and of being outside, whether she was in Texas, Maryland or Mexico. After moving to San Francisco as an adult, Ynes began exploring the surrounding redwood forests, and she wanted to know more. At the time, it was rare for women to go to college, especially women in their fifties. But at fifty-one, she persisted in studying botany at UC Berkeley. Over her career, she traveled across the Americas and collected more than 145,000 specimens of plants, which, decades later, scientists are still studying. At least fifty of the specimens Ynes discovered are named after her.

I don't think there is any place in the world where a woman can't venture.

When GRACE HOPPER was born, most
mathematicians were men (and still are today). But Grace earned
a PhD in mathematics and became an assistant professor of math
at Vassar College. Then she joined the US Naval Reserve during
World War II and began working with a very early computer
named Mark I; she was one of the first people ever to program
it. When a moth got caught in its circuits, Grace called it a bug,
creating a term we still use today for unexpected computer
problems. Some male computer scientists didn't believe she
could create a program that translated words into numbers, but
she persisted and showed she could. Her work led to the
invention of programming languages. For all of her contributions,
she's sometimes called "Amazing Grace."

If you do something once, people will call it an accident. If you do it twice, they call it a coincidence. But do it a third time and you've just proven a natural law!

COBOL

MOTHER OF COMPUTING

As a teenager, ROSALIND FRANKLIN knew she wanted to be a scientist, so she studied hard to become a chemist. While Rosalind's early work was on carbon, her later work focused on viruses. She and one of her students discovered that there were two different forms of DNA, our genetic code, and she took a photograph using her X-ray technology to prove it. A male scientist who didn't like Rosalind showed her work to two other scientists, James Watson and Francis Crick, who were also studying DNA. Watson and Crick based their DNA model on Rosalind's work, and when they were awarded the Nobel Prize in Medicine, they failed to give her the credit she deserved. Still, **she persisted** in continuing her research, and her work is still being used today by scientists investigating many viruses, including the virus that causes COVID-19.

Science and everyday life cannot and should not be separated.

GLADYS WEST knew she had to get a good education to realize her dreams. Her family didn't have much money, so **she persisted** in working hard, became her high school's valedictorian, got a scholarship to Virginia State College (now Virginia State University) and earned her degree in math. She was hired by the US Navy and focused her work on the study of Pluto's and Neptune's orbits, and found out that Pluto made two orbits around the sun in the time it took Neptune to make three. She then worked on the Seasat, the first satellite that could successfully sense oceans. Using that information, Gladys created a more exact model of Earth's surface. Her work is the basis for GPS, the direction system used around the world; so we can all thank Gladys for helping us not get lost.

When you're working every day, you're not thinking,
"What impact is this going to have on the world?"
You're thinking, "I've got to get this right."

As a child, JANE GOODALL loved animals and dreamed of traveling to Africa to live and study the animals she had only seen in books. When she was twenty-six years old, Jane moved to Gombe Stream Chimpanzee Reserve (now Gombe National Park) in Tanzania, to start her own research camp and study chimpanzees. Because she did not have a PhD, some people doubted that she could make any research contributions. She persisted and discovered many new facts about chimpanzees, including that they make and use tools, which no one had known before. Even after her groundbreaking work, some male scientists dismissed her findings because she was a young woman. Six decades after Jane moved to Gombe, she and the Jane Goodall Institute continue to research chimpanzees, work to protect them and teach young scientists across the globe.

Every one of us makes a difference . . .
How we act each day can begin
to change the world.

As a girl in Hong Kong, FLOSSIE WONG-STAAL went to an American-run school. Thinking it might help her succeed, her parents and teachers encouraged her to change her name from Wong Yee Ching to something that sounded more American. Her father suggested Flossie after a recent typhoon, perhaps believing that his daughter could take the world by storm. When she moved to Los Angeles for college, **she persisted** in her love of science. Flossie was one of the first scientists to study HIV, a disease that attacks the immune system, our body's defense against germs. Her work led to the development of medications to fight HIV. Flossie's research also helped us better understand cancer and other viruses, including COVID-19. Millions of people around the world today are alive because of Flossie.

It adds to the joy of discovery to know that your work may make a difference in people's lives.

As a toddler, TEMPLE GRANDIN didn't speak, and she was later diagnosed with autism. Even after she did start to talk, school was challenging for Temple because other kids made fun of her for being different, but **she persisted**. After spending time on her aunt's ranch, she later realized that the animals she was around felt the same fear and sensitivity to sound and touch that she did. After completing a PhD in animal science, Temple dedicated her life to improving the living conditions of cows and bulls on ranches and farms. Today, the system Temple developed to check how well animals are treated is the standard across the United States. Temple's research, writing and speaking about autism has helped empower children to know they, too, can succeed, no matter how their brains work.

What has given my life meaning is more than doing science; it's helping people solve problems using science. Doing something that makes a difference with what I've learned.

As a girl growing up in Iraq, ZAHA HADID went with her family to visit ancient Sumerian cities, which inspired her passion for buildings and her studies in mathematics and architecture. Although her professors in England thought she was a brilliant student, and though women were working as architects in Iraq at the time, some people in England thought that women weren't capable of imagining new spaces. She persisted and opened her own firm. Over her career, she built spectacular museums, the aquatics center for the 2012 London Olympics and more. Zaha became the first woman to receive the Pritzker Architecture Prize and the Royal Institute of British Architects' Royal Gold Medal in her own right. But though she was the first, she will probably not be the last; close to half of architecture students in the United States today are women.

I used to not like being called a woman architect. But I see the incredible amount of need from other women for reassurance that it could be done, so I don't mind that at all.

As a girl, ELLEN OCHOA didn't know any engineers or scientists. Then she became one, concentrating on optics, the study of how light behaves, and designing computer systems. She never dared to dream of being an astronaut because she didn't know women could go to space. That changed when she saw Sally Ride orbiting Earth in a space shuttle. She persisted in chasing her new dream, joining NASA as a research engineer and then going to space four times, spending nearly one thousand hours in orbit. After Ellen retired from space travel, she became the first Hispanic director of the Johnson Space Center, which trains future astronauts and serves as NASA's mission control to keep them safe.

Don't be afraid to reach for the stars.

When **MARI COPENY** was eight years old, she knew that the water in her hometown, Flint, Michigan, wasn't safe to drink or bathe in. On a trip to Washington, DC, she wrote to President Obama asking him to meet; he responded by actually coming to Flint to see the situation firsthand. **DR. MONA HANNA-ATTISHA**, a pediatrician, helped to uncover that the water, which Flint families like Mari's were using, had high levels of lead, a poison that can harm kids' brains, and that state political leaders had lied about it. Mari and Dr. Mona worked to raise broad awareness about the crisis in Flint and on solutions to protect public health. **They persisted**, demanding safer water for their community and accountability for the leaders who had lied. Today, Dr. Mona continues to care for Flint's youngest in her clinic and through the organization Flint Kids. Mari works with Flint Kids, too, and is producing her own water filter, all while still in school.

You're never too young or too small to change the world.
—Mari Copeny

The world . . . should be full of people raising their voices, using their power and presence, standing up for what's right.
—Dr. Mona Hanna-Attisha

AUTUMN PELTIER, GRETA THUNBERG and ELIZABETH WANJIRU WATHUTI are three young activists who want to explain to the world what science tells us about how and why our Earth is warming and our weather is changing. Even though some people have a hard time believing young women, **these three have persisted** in fighting for our future. Elizabeth planted her first tree when she was seven. Today, she runs the Green Generation Initiative, which has planted more than thirty thousand trees. Autumn began her clean-water advocacy for First Nations communities years before she became the chief water commissioner for the Anishinabek Nation at age fourteen. When Greta started spending weekdays outside the Swedish Parliament calling for stronger action on climate change at the age of fifteen, she was alone. The next year, millions of people on a "school strike for climate" demanded more action from their governments. She's been named one of the most powerful people in the world.

We showed that we are united and that we,
young people, are unstoppable.
—Greta Thunberg

If you don't act, we will!
—Elizabeth Wanjiru Wathuti

No child should grow up not knowing what clean
water is or never know what running water is.
—Autumn Peltier

So if anyone ever tells you that women can't be scientists, if anyone ever tells you women's ideas aren't good enough or smart enough, don't listen to them. Women can be anything they want to be and make the impossible possible, just like these scientists did.

They persisted and so should you.